LOGOS CURSIVE
Book 1: The Alphabet

Published by Logos Press
an imprint of Canon Press
P.O. Box 8729, Moscow, Idaho 83843
800.488.2034 | logospressonline.com

B.J. Loyd, *Logos Cursive, Book 1: The Alphabet*
Copyright © 2019 by B.J. Loyd

Cover design by James Engerbretson.
Illustrations by Mark Beauchamp.
Interior design and exercise sentences by Valerie Anne Bost.

Printed in the United States of America.

All rights reserved. No part of this publication may be reproduced, stored in a retrieval system, or transmitted in any form by any means, electronic, mechanical, photocopy, recording, or otherwise, without prior permission of the author, except as provided by USA copyright law.

Library of Congress Cataloging-in-Publication Data forthcoming.

19 20 21 22 23 24 25 26 27 28 29   10 9 8 7 6 5 4 3 2 1

Logos Cursive
Book 1: The Alphabet

B.J. LOYD

AN IMPRINT OF CANON PRESS | MOSCOW, IDAHO

Schedule

Dear Teacher,

Welcome to *Logos Cursive, Book 1: The Alphabet*. This schedule will help you teach your second graders cursive over the course of a semester.

WEEK	ASSIGNMENT
1	Printing Review 1–5
2	Printing Review 6–10
3	Exercises 1–5
4	Exercises 6–10
5	Exercises 11–15
6	Exercises 16–20
7	Exercises 21–25
8	Exercises 26–30
9	Exercises 31–35
10	Exercises 36–40
11	Exercises 41–45
12	Exercises 46–50
13	Exercises 51–55
14	Exercises 56–60
15	Exercises 61–65
16	Exercises 66–70

Name: _____

Let's review printed letters. Copy the letter at the beginning of each line. Use the blank lines for extra practice.

A

a

B

b

C

c

Name: _____

Let's review printed letters. Copy the letter at the beginning of each line. Use the blank lines for extra practice.

D

d

E

e

F

f

Name: _____

Let's review printed letters. Copy the letter at the beginning of each line. Use the blank lines for extra practice.

G

g

H

h

I

i

Book 1: The Alphabet

Printing Review 3

Name: _____

Let's review printed letters. Copy the letter at the beginning of each line. Use the blank lines for extra practice.

J

j

K

k

L

l

Name: _____

Let's review printed letters. Copy the letter at the beginning of each line. Use the blank lines for extra practice.

M

m

N

n

O

o

Book 1: The Alphabet

Name: _____

Let's review printed letters. Copy the letter at the beginning of each line. Use the blank lines for extra practice.

P

p

Q

q

R

r

Name: _____

Let's review printed letters. Copy the letter at the beginning of each line. Use the blank lines for extra practice.

S

s

T

t

U

u

Book 1: The Alphabet

Printing Review 7

Name: _____

Let's review printed letters. Copy the letter at the beginning of each line. Use the blank lines for extra practice.

V

v

W

w

X

x

Printing Review 8   Logos Cursive

Name: _____

Let's review printed letters. Copy the letter at the beginning of each line. Use the blank lines for extra practice. Then copy the sentence.

Y

y

Z

z

The five boxing wizards jump quickly.

Book 1: The Alphabet

Name: _____

Copy the sentences.

Pack my red box with five dozen quality jugs.

Zeb's happy cow gave quarts of jinxed milk.

Name: _____

Start each **l** at the bottom, and trace the dotted line.

l *l l l l l l l l l l l*

l *l l l l l l l l l l l*

l *l l l l l l l l l l l*

Now make a whole row.

l *l*

Let's try two linked together.

ll *ll ll ll ll ll ll ll*

ll

ladder

Book 1: The Alphabet

Exercise 1

Name: _____

Start each **h** at the bottom, and trace the dotted line.

Now make a whole row.

Let's try linking letters together.

hand

Exercise 2

Logos Cursive

Name: _____

Start each **k** at the bottom, and trace the dotted line.

Now make a whole row.

Let's try linking letters together.

kangaroo

Book 1: The Alphabet

Exercise 3

Name: _____

Start each **t** at the bottom, and trace the dotted line. When you get to the top, trace back down to the big dot.

t ....

Next, lift your pencil and make the cross bar.

t ....

When you link a **t**, write all the letters, and then add the cross bar.

tt ....

th ....

lth ....

lth

ht ....

ht

teapot

Logos Cursive

Name: _____

Start each **i** at the bottom, and trace the dotted line.

Always add the dot last.

Now make a whole row.

Dotting an i is like crossing a t. Link all of the letters, and then add the dot.

You now know enough letters to write real words in cursive. Trace each word, and then write it by yourself.

igloo

Book 1: The Alphabet

Name: _____

Start each **u** at the bottom, and trace the dotted line.

Now make a whole row.

Link letters and write whole words.

uu

ut

hut

hulk

tutu

utensils

Exercise 6

Logos Cursive

Name: _____

Start each **e** at the bottom, and trace the dotted line.

e e e e e e e e e e e e e e e e e

e e e e e e e e e e e e e e e e e e

Now make a whole row.

e .... *e*

Link letters and write whole words.

ee ee ee ee ee ee ee ee ee ee

he he he he he he he he he

the the the the the the the

hike hike hike
hike hike hike

little little little

emu

Book 1: The Alphabet

Exercise 7

Name: _____

Now we have the first letter with a tail. Start each **j** at the base line, and trace the dotted line.

Always add the dot last.

Make a whole row.

Link letters and write whole words.

jellyfish

jet

jut

Exercise 8

Logos Cursive

Name: _____

Start each **p** at the baseline, and trace the dotted line.

p ....

Now make a whole row.

p

Link letters and write whole words.

pp pp pp pp pep pep pep

pie pie pie put put put

pile pile pile

hip hip hip hip

keep keep keep

plant

Book 1: The Alphabet

Exercise 9

Name: _____

Start each **a** at the bottom, and trace the dotted line.

a *i* *i* *i* *i* *i* *i* *i* *i* *i* *i* *i* *i* *i* *i*

a *c* *c* *c* *c* *c* *c* *c* *c* *c* *c* *c* *c* *c* *c*

a *a* *a* *a* *a* *a* *a* *a* *a* *a* *a* *a* *a* *a* *a*

Now make a whole row.

a   *a*

Link letters and write whole words.

aa aa aa aa aa aa

ape ape ape ape ape ape

take take take

anchor

apple apple apple

pail pail pail

Exercise 10   Logos Cursive

Name: _____

Start each **d** at the bottom, and trace the dotted line.

Now make a whole row.

Link letters and write whole words.

dolphin

Book 1: The Alphabet Exercise 11

Name: _____

Start each **c** at the bottom, and trace the dotted line.

Now make a whole row.

Link letters and write whole words.

camel

Exercise 12

Logos Cursive

Name: _____

Start each **m** at the bottom, and trace the dotted line.

Now make a whole row.

Link letters and write whole words.

mm mm me me me

mat mat mile mile

jam jam jam

emu emu emu

mouse

Book 1: The Alphabet

Exercise 13

Name: _____

Start each **n** at the bottom, and trace the dotted line.

Now make a whole row.

Link letters and write whole words.

nn nap nap nap
net net net pain pain
din din din nice nice

nuthatch

tuned tuned
tuned tuned

Exercise 14   Logos Cursive

Name: _____

Start each **x** at the baseline, and trace the dotted line.

Next, lift your pencil and cross the x.

Now make a whole row.

Link letters and write whole words.

x-ray

Book 1: The Alphabet

Exercise 15

Name: _____

Start each **g** at the baseline, and trace the dotted line.

Now make a whole row.

Link letters and write whole words.

goat

Exercise 16

Logos Cursive

Name: _____

Start each **y** at the baseline, and trace the dotted line.

Now make a whole row.

Link letters and write whole words.

ya ya ya ya ya ya

yet yet yet lay lay lay

yummy yummy

yip yip yip yip

clay clay clay

yarn

Book 1: The Alphabet

Exercise 17

Name: _____

Start each **q** at the bottom, and trace the dotted line.

[tracing rows for cursive q]

Now make a whole row.

[practice row for q]

Link letters and write whole words.

qq *[tracing: qu qu qu qu qu]*

[tracing: quilt quilt quilt quilt]

quarter

[tracing: quad quad]

[tracing: quad equal]

[tracing: equal equal]

Exercise 18   Logos Cursive

Name: _____

Start each **o** at the bottom, and trace the dotted line.

Now make a whole row.

Link letters and write whole words.

oo oo on on on on

oat oat oat old old old

coil coil coil

loop loop loop

joy joy joy

owl

Book 1: The Alphabet

Exercise 19

Name: _____

Start each **w** at the bottom, and trace the dotted line.

Now make a whole row.

Link letters and write whole words.

water

Exercise 20

Logos Cursive

Name: _____

Start each **b** at the bottom, and trace the dotted line.

[tracing rows of cursive b]

Now make a whole row.

[tracing row with cursive b]

Link letters and write whole words.

bb bb bb be be be be

bit bit bit bug bug bug

bob bob bob

baby baby

bubble bubble

bear

Book 1: The Alphabet

Exercise 21

Name: _____

Start each **v** at the bottom, and trace the dotted line.

Now make a whole row.

Link letters and write whole words.

violin

Exercise 22   Logos Cursive

Name: _____

Start each **z** at the bottom, and trace the dotted line.

Now make a whole row.

Link letters and write whole words.

maze

Book 1: The Alphabet

Exercise 23

Name: _____

Start each **s** at the bottom, and trace the dotted line.

Now make a whole row.

Link letters and write whole words.

sit sit sit sap sap sap

sew sew sew sew

sums sums sums

shush shush

sock

Exercise 24   Logos Cursive

Name: _____

Start each **r** at the bottom, and trace the dotted line.

Now make a whole row.

Link letters and write whole words.

r r ra ra re re re

rid rid rid rug rug rug

roses roses roses

rare rare rare

peer peer peer

run

Book 1: The Alphabet

Exercise 25

Name: _____

Start each **f** at the baseline, and trace the dotted line.

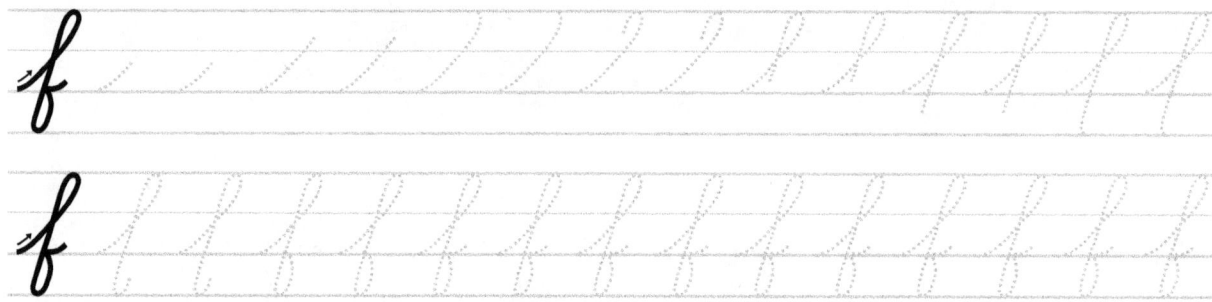

Make a whole row.

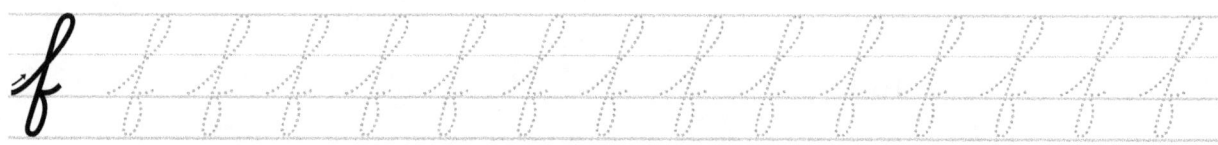

Link letters and write whole words.

fox

Exercise 26 — Logos Cursive

Name: _____

Start each **A** at the top, and trace the dotted line.

a ⋯ *aaaaaaaaaa*

Trace each line, and then write it on your own in the blank spaces. Connect the capital **A** to the following letters.

Asher Always Ate Apples

Asher Always Ate Apples

Ada Aids Abe's Aardvark

Ada Aids Abe's Aardvark

Aaron Acted

Aaron Acted

aardvark

Name: _____

Start each **C** at the top, and trace the dotted line.

C C C C C C C C C C C C C

Trace each line, and then write it on your own in the blank spaces. Connect the capital **C** to the following letters.

Cyrus Creates Crazy Cities

Cyrus Creates Crazy Cities

Christy Cut Crisp Carrots

Christy Cut Crisp Carrots

columbine

Cooper Chuckled

Cooper Chuckled

Exercise 28   Logos Cursive

Name: _____

Start each **E** at the top, and trace the dotted line.

𝓔

Trace each line, and then write it on your own in the blank spaces. Connect the capital **E** to the following letters.

Edmund Eats Eight Eggs

Edmund Eats Eight Eggs

Eileen Exits Each Elevator

Eileen Exits Each Elevator

Eve Entertains

Eve Entertains

eggs

Book 1: The Alphabet   Exercise 29

Name: _____

Start each **O** at the top, and trace the dotted line.

O O O O O O O O O

Trace each line, and then write it on your own in the blank spaces. Don't connect the capital **O** to the following letters.

Opal Often Opens Oreos

Opal Often Opens Oreos

Owen Ordered Oatmeal

Owen Ordered Oatmeal

Otto Obeyed

Otto Obeyed

oven

Exercise 30

Logos Cursive

Name: _____

Start each **H** at the top, and trace the dotted line.

Trace each line, and then write it on your own in the blank spaces. Don't connect the capital **H** to the following letters.

Henry Hit Hard Homers

Henry Hit Hard Homers

Heather Hates Her Hat

Heather Hates Her Hat

Hello, Hobbits

Hello, Hobbits

hat

Book 1: The Alphabet · · · Exercise 31

Name: _____

Start each **K** at the top, and trace the first dotted line. Lift your pencil and start again at the top for the second part.

K K K K K K K K K

Trace each line, and then write it on your own in the blank spaces. Connect the capital **K** to the following letters.

Kate Kisses Kind Kittens

Kate Kisses Kind Kittens

Ken Kicked Kody's Knees

Ken Kicked Kody's Knees

kitten

Kelly Kept Knobs

Kelly Kept Knobs

Exercise 32   Logos Cursive

Name: _____

Start each **N** at the top, and trace the dotted line.

𝒏

Trace each line, and then write it on your own in the blank spaces. Connect the capital **N** to the following letters.

Nancy Never Nags Nick

Nancy Never Nags Nick

Nate Needed Ninety Nails

Nate Needed Ninety Nails

Nina Nudges Ned

Nina Nudges Ned

nails

Book 1: The Alphabet

Exercise 33

Name: _____

Start each **M** at the top, and trace the dotted line.

M M M M M M M M M

Trace each line, and then write it on your own in the blank spaces. Connect the capital **M** to the following letters.

Moses Must Mind Mama

Moses Must Mind Mama

Mari Made Many Moose

Mari Made Many Moose

Meg Munches

Meg Munches

moose

Name: _____

Start each **U** at the top, and trace the dotted line.

U U U U U U U U U U

Trace each line, and then write it on your own in the blank spaces. Connect the capital **U** to the following letters.

Ursula Upsets Unicorns

Ursula Upsets Unicorns

Ulrich Undoes Umbrellas

Ulrich Undoes Umbrellas

Ulysses Urged

Ulysses Urged

umbrella

Book 1: The Alphabet

Exercise 35

Name: _____

Start each **V** at the top, and trace the dotted line.

𝒱

Trace each line, and then write it on your own in the blank spaces. Don't connect the capital **V** to the following letters.

Vera Values Vivid Verbs

Vera Values Vivid Verbs

Victor Viewed Video

Victor Viewed Video

vulture

Valerie Vexes Van

Valerie Vexes Van

Name: _____

Start each **W** at the top, and trace the dotted line.

W

Trace each line, and then write it on your own in the blank spaces. Don't connect the capital **W** to the following letters.

Wade Woke Wary Wrens

Wade Woke Wary Wrens

Wanda Wondered Wildly

Wanda Wondered Wildly

Wes Whistles

Wes Whistles

wren

Book 1: The Alphabet — Exercise 37

Name: _____

Start each **Y** at the top, and trace the dotted line.

Y *Y Y Y Y Y Y Y Y*

Trace each line, and then write it on your own in the blank spaces. Connect the capital **Y** to the following letters.

Yates Yipped Yesterday

Yates Yipped Yesterday

Yolanda's Yak Yells Yes

Yolanda's Yak Yells Yes

Yvette Yodels

Yvette Yodels

yak

Exercise 38   Logos Cursive

Name: _____

Start each **T** at the bottom, and trace the first dotted line. Lift your pencil and start again at the top for the second part.

Trace each line, and then write it on your own in the blank spaces. Don't connect the capital **T** to the following letters.

tablets

Book 1: The Alphabet

Exercise 39

Name: _____

Start each **F** at the top, and trace the dotted line. Lift your pencil and start again at the top for the second part. Finally, make the cross bar.

F F F F F F F F

Trace each line, and then write it on your own in the blank spaces. Don't connect the capital **F** to the following letters.

Fred Farms Fat Frog

Fred Farms Fat Frog

Fiona Fit Fall Fashion

Fiona Fit Fall Fashion

frog

Felicity Forgave

Felicity Forgave

Exercise 40 — Logos Cursive

Name: _____

Start each **B** at the top, and trace the dotted line.

B B B B B B B B B B B

Trace each line, and then write it on your own in the blank spaces. Don't connect the capital **B** to the following letters.

Becky Bored Busy Bees

Becky Bored Busy Bees

Brian Bindi Bad Books

Brian Bindi Bad Books

Bobby Bounced

Bobby Bounced

ball

Book 1: The Alphabet

Exercise 41

Name: _____

Start each **P** at the top, and trace the dotted line.

P *P P P P P P P P P P*

Trace each line, and then write it on your own in the blank spaces. Don't connect the capital **P** to the following letters.

Patti Picks Pretty Peaches

Patti Picks Pretty Peaches

Paul Paid Pop's Pelican

Paul Paid Pop's Pelican

pelican

Prudence Paced

Prudence Paced

Exercise 42

Logos Cursive

Name: _____

Start each **R** at the top, and trace the dotted line.

R R R R R R R R R R

Trace each line, and then write it on your own in the blank spaces. Connect the capital **R** to the following letters.

Rupert Romped Robustly

Rupert Romped Robustly

Rory Raised Red Rabbits

Rory Raised Red Rabbits

Rita Rhymes

Rita Rhymes

rabbit

Book 1: The Alphabet

Exercise 43

Name: _____

Start each **G** at the bottom, and trace the dotted line.

Trace each line, and then write it on your own in the blank spaces. Don't connect the capital **G** to the following letters.

Gloria Got Great Guests

Gloria Got Great Guests

Gene Gave Gail Globes

Gene Gave Gail Globes

Gil Grew Grapes

Gil Grew Grapes

globe

Exercise 44   Logos Cursive

Name: _____

Start each **S** at the bottom, and trace the dotted line.

Trace each line, and then write it on your own in the blank spaces. Don't connect the capital **S** to the following letters.

Sat Swung Six Swords

Sat Swung Six Swords

Suzie Sat Still Sweetly

Suzie Sat Still Sweetly

Shad Sips Soda

Shad Sips Soda

sword

Book 1: The Alphabet

Exercise 45

Name: _____

Start each **I** in the middle, and trace the dotted line.

I

Trace each line, and then write it on your own in the blank spaces. Connect the capital **I** to the following letters.

Isabel Is Iddy Impish

Isabel Is Iddy Impish

Ian Irks Icky Insects

Ian Irks Icky Insects

iguana

Ida Inspires

Ida Inspires

Exercise 46 — Logos Cursive

Name: _____

There are two ways to make a **Q**. For the first way, start at the top, and trace the dotted line.

Q Q Q Q Q Q Q Q Q Q

For the second way, write an **O**. Then lift your pencil and add a tail.

Q Q Q Q Q Q Q Q Q Q Q

Trace each line, and then write it on your own in the blank spaces. Try both ways, and then pick the one you like best. Connect the capital **Q** to the following letters.

Quinn Questions Quails

Quincy Quacked Quietly

Quintus Quit

Quintus Quit

quail

Book 1: The Alphabet

Exercise 47

Name: _____

Start each **Z** at the top, and trace the dotted line.

Z

Trace each line, and then write it on your own in the blank spaces. Connect the capital **F** to the following letters.

Zeke Zapped Zero Zebras

Zeke Zapped Zero Zebras

Zachary Zoomed Zestily

Zachary Zoomed Zestily

zebra

Zara Zigzags

Zara Zigzags

Exercise 48   Logos Cursive

Name: _____

Start each **D** at the top, and trace the dotted line.

D D D D D D D D D

Trace each line, and then write it on your own in the blank spaces. Don't connect the capital **D** to the following letters.

Deb Dahi Daintily

Deb Dahi Daintily

Dan's Dog Digs Daily

Dan's Dog Digs Daily

Diane Dazzles

Diane Dazzles

dog

Book 1: The Alphabet

Exercise 49

Name: _____

Start each **J** a little below the baseline, and trace the dotted line.

Trace each line, and then write it on your own in the blank spaces. Connect the capital **J** to the following letters.

Janice Juggles Jumbo Jets

Jon Jab's Joe's Jutting Jaw

jet

Jill Jinxed Jed

Exercise 50

Logos Cursive

Name: _____

Start each **X** at the top, and trace the dotted line. Lift your pencil and start again at the top to make the second part.

𝒳   𝒳 𝒳 𝒳 𝒳 𝒳 𝒳 𝒳

Trace each line, and then write it on your own in the blank spaces. Connect the capital **X** to the following letters and cross the **X** when you are done.

Xenia X es Xylophones

Xenia X es Xylophones

Xanthe X-rayed Xavier

Xanthe X-rayed Xavier

Xan Xeroxed

Xan Xeroxed

xylophone

Book 1: The Alphabet

Exercise 51

Name: _____

Start each **L** below the top line, and trace the dotted line.

L L L L L L L L L

L L L L L L L L L

L L L L L L L L L

Trace each line, and then write it on your own in the blank spaces. Connect the capital **L** to the following letters.

Lyn Likes Loud Llamas

Lyn Likes Loud Llamas

Larry Lost Limp Lettuce

Luke Loves Lizzy

llama

Exercise 52

Logos Cursive

Name: _____

Trace and then neatly copy.

Fruit of the Spirit

love

joy

peace

patience

kindness

goodness

faithfulness

gentleness

self-control

Name: _____

Trace and then neatly copy.

But the fruit of the

Spirit is love, joy, peace,

patience, kindness,

goodness, faithfulness,

gentleness, self-control;

against such things

there is no law.

Galatians 5:22-23

Name: _____

Trace and then neatly copy.

So, whether you eat or

drink, or whatever you

do, do it all to the

glory of God.

1 Corinthians 10:31

Name: _____

Trace and then neatly copy.

Therefore, since we have been justified by faith, we have peace with God through our Lord Jesus Christ. Romans 5:1

Name: _____

Trace and then neatly copy.

Do all things without

grumbling or disputing.

Philippians 2:14

Name: _____

Trace and then neatly copy.

For God so loved the

world, that he gave his

only Son, that whoever

believes in him should

not perish but have

Book 1: The Alphabet   Exercise 58

Name: _____

eternal life. John 3:16

Exercise 58 Logos Cursive

Name: _____

Trace and then neatly copy.

Keep your tongue from

evil and your lips

from speaking deceit.

Turn away from evil

and do good; seek peace

Name: _____

and pursue it.

Psalm 34:13-14

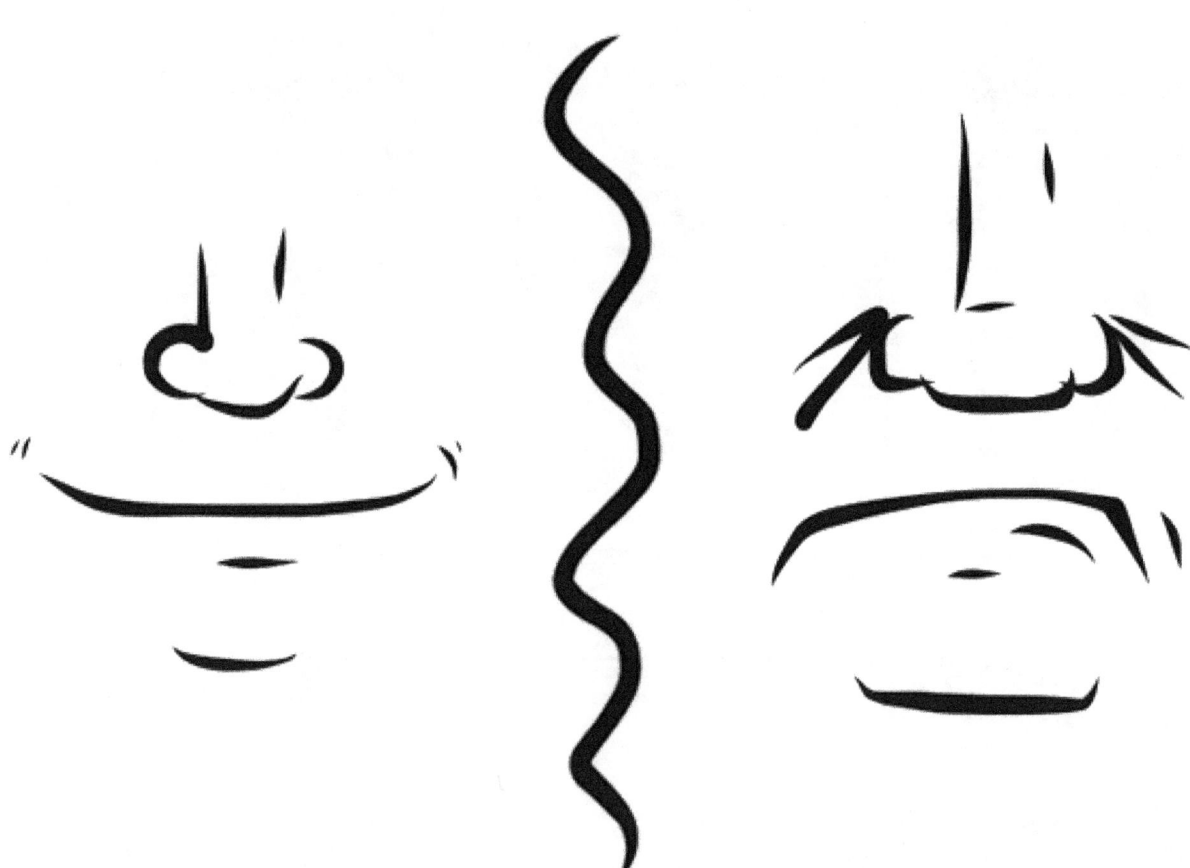

Exercise 59

Logos Cursive

Name: _____

Trace and then neatly copy.

Rejoice in the Lord

always; again I will

say, rejoice.

Philippians 4:4

Name: _____

Trace and then neatly copy.

If we confess our

sins, He is faithful

and just to forgive

us our sins and to

cleanse us from all

Exercise 61 — Logos Cursive

Name: _____

unrighteousness.

1 John 1:8b-9

Book 1: The AlphabetExercise 61

Name: _____

Trace and then neatly copy.

And as you wish that

others would do to

you, do so to them.

Luke 6:31

Name: _____

Trace and then neatly copy.

Let every person be

quick to hear, slow

to speak, slow to

anger; for the anger of

man does not produce

Name: _____

the righteousness of

God. James 1:19b-20

Name: _____

Trace and then neatly copy.

Children, obey your parents in everything, for this pleases the Lord.

Colossians 3:20

Name: _____

Trace and then neatly copy.

But Jesus said, "Let the

little children come to

me and do not hinder

them, for to such

belongs the kingdom

Name: _____

of heaven."

Matthew 19:14

Book 1: The Alphabet

Exercise 65

Name: _____

Trace and then neatly copy.

But be doers of the

Word, and not hearers

only, deceiving

yourselves. James 1:22

Name: _____

Trace and then neatly copy.

He himself bore our

sins in his body on

the tree, that we might

die to sin and live to

righteousness. By his

Name: _____

wounds you have been

healed. 1 Peter 2:24

Exercise 67 — Logos Cursive

Name: _____

Trace and then neatly copy.

Be kind to one another,

tenderhearted, forgiving

one another, as God in

Christ forgave you.

Ephesians 4:32

Name: _____

Trace and then neatly copy.

And whatever you ask

in prayer, you will

receive, if you have

faith. Matthew 21:22

Name: _____

Trace and then neatly copy.

Do not be alarmed.

You seek Jesus of

Nazareth, who was

crucified. He has risen;

he is not here. See the

Name: _____

place where they laid

him. Mark 16:6b

www.ingramcontent.com/pod-product-compliance
Lightning Source LLC
Chambersburg PA
CBHW050455110426
42743CB00017B/3379